M.R. JOHNSON

Small Business Growth Strategies for 2025

Boost profits, make savvy Investment choices, lead a high performance team, know what your business is worth

Copyright © 2024 by M.R. Johnson

All rights reserved. No part of this publication may be reproduced, stored or transmitted in any form or by any means, electronic, mechanical, photocopying, recording, scanning, or otherwise without written permission from the publisher. It is illegal to copy this book, post it to a website, or distribute it by any other means without permission.

M.R. Johnson asserts the moral right to be identified as the author of this work.

M.R. Johnson has no responsibility for the persistence or accuracy of URLs for external or third-party Internet Websites referred to in this publication and does not guarantee that any content on such Websites is, or will remain, accurate or appropriate.

Designations used by companies to distinguish their products are often claimed as trademarks. All brand names and product names used in this book and on its cover are trade names, service marks, trademarks and registered trademarks of their respective owners. The publishers and the book are not associated with any product or vendor mentioned in this book. None of the companies referenced within the book have endorsed the book.

First edition

This book was professionally typeset on Reedsy. Find out more at reedsy.com

"Thinking is the hardest work there is which is probably the reason so few engage in it." Henry Ford

"Blessed are those who find wisdom, those who gain understanding, for she is more profitable than silver and yields better returns than gold." Proverbs 3:13-14

Contents

Acknowledgments ii
Introduction 1
1 Embracing the Future, AI & Business operating systems... 5
2 Leading The Millennial Wave, Continuous Growth,... 10
3 Deeper Dive, Leveraging Operating Systems with AI, Maximum... 19
4 A-Players, Developing and Retaining Talent 27
5 The Power of a "Next Gen Engaged Culture" and How to Get It 31
6 Leveraging Good Coaching for Enhanced Performance 36
7 Assessing Your Business's Value in the Eyes of Investors 40
8 Charting a Path to Future Success 45
9 Conclusion Story & Contact information 47

Acknowledgments

I want to thank Dr. Clark Barshinger and Tony Orsini. Two great friends, mentors and colleagues. Tony founded his company, with a card table and fold out chair, and grew Orsini Healthcare to a $500 million dollar business. He was my first CEO Round table member and client. He is a great friend to this day.

Clark and I met when he came to one of my investment banking functions and became a client. His wisdom and life's work have impacted the lives of many for the better. Especially me. He continues to be my mentor, coach and friend after 24 years. Clark Barshinger is the founder and CEO of Cherry Hill Counseling centers and has over 50 clinicians in the Chicago land area with multiple offices.

I also want to thank Bill George. He was CEO of Medtronic at the time, 2001, and I saw him speak at the Global Leadership Summit about a new type of Master's program. It was based on Emotional intelligence and your true leadership talents. He was incubating the program at Bethel college in the Minneapolis area. That is where Medtronic is located and the company he was CEO of from 1991 to 2001. As I heard him speak, I knew I had to get into that program. I did and got my Masters in Transformational leadership in 2008. Forever grateful to Bill.

Bill George is now an executive fellow at Harvard Business School, where he has been a Professor of Management Practice and Senior Fellow teaching leadership since 2004.

I am also grateful to the following authors and business coaches for their insights and wisdom, which have shaped my approach and understanding. I encourage you to explore their works and consider adding them to your library, as they have been instrumental in my own development:

- *Great By Choice* by Jim Collins
- *Investor's Business Daily*
- *Pinnacle: Five Principles that Take Your business to the Top of the Mountain* By Greg Cleary and Steve Preda
- *True North: Discover Your Authentic Leadership*, by Bill George
- *The Seven Habits of Highly Effective People* by Stephen R. Covey
- *The Speed of Trust* by Stephen M.R. Covey
- *The Advantage* by Patrick Lencioni
- *The Five Dysfunctions of a Team* by Patrick Lencioni
- *Crucial Conversations* by Joseph Grenny, Kerry Patterson, Ron McMillan, Al Switzler, and Emily Gregory
- *Death by Meeting* by Patrick Lencioni
- *Scaling Up* by Verne Harnish
- *Traction* by Gino Wickman
- *What the Heck is EOS* by Gino Wickman and Tom Bouwer
- *Strengths Based Leadership* by Tom Rath and Barry Conchie
- *Earn It* by Jill E. Young
- *Start With Why* by Simon Sinek
- *Lessons For Living: What Only Adversity Can Teach You* by Phil Stutz
- *The Tools: 5 Tools to Help You Find Courage, Creativity, and Willpower—and Inspire You to Live Your Life in Forward Motion* by Phil Stutz and Barry Michels

Thank you to these authors for their dedication to knowledge and growth. Your work continues to enlighten and guide leaders across the globe.

Introduction

A little bit about me and why some businesses win and others don't.

This little book you have in your hand, has the potential to radically transform your business. All you must do is ACT! Act on just 1 or 2 of the tools and concepts in this book and you can add anywhere from an extra $30k per year to $1mm per year. This is a fact. I'm an investment banker and business coach. I have seen these tools help thousands of businesses expand in powerful ways. So, what I want to challenge you to do, is develop that **"Sense of Urgency"** for 2025, that you will act on some of these ideas. Any one of them can help your business. But there are 2 that will provide the biggest return for the effort. I'll let you discern which that will be for you.

Let me just share with you what the best leaders of companies do, disciplines they follow, that you can follow too. This is from *"Investors Business Daily"*. Probably one of the best publications in the world for aspiring business owners. These are facts because IBD interviews the leaders of the companies that they invest in. Then sharing those interviews in their publication in the *"Leaders and Success" section*. They have spent years analyzing leaders and successful people. They observed ten traits, when combined, can turn dreams into reality.

Here they are:

SMALL BUSINESS GROWTH STRATEGIES FOR 2025

1-**How you think is everything**: Always think positive, think success not failure. Beware of a negative environment.

2-**Decide upon your true dreams and goals**: Write down specific goals and develop a plan to reach them.

3-**Take Action**: Goals are nothing without action. Don't be afraid to get started. Just do it!

4- **Never stop learning**: Go back to school, read books. Get training and acquire skills.

5- **Be persistent and work hard:** Success is a marathon. Not a sprint. Never give up.

6- **Learn to analyze details:** Get all the facts, all the input. Learn from your mistakes.

7- **Focus your time and money:** Don't let other people or things distract you.

8- **Don't be afraid to innovate, be different:** Following the herd is a sure way to mediocrity.

9- **Deal and communicate with people effectively:** No person is an island. Learn to understand and motivate.

10- **Be honest and dependable:** Otherwise 1-9 won't matter.

Leaders are no different from you and me. They just know what the high priority, high payoff items are and put all their focus on them and their family. You can do this too! Set your resolution for 2025!

In this book, I present practical strategies and actionable steps that you can apply immediately. These steps are designed to **deliver an *excellent return on your time and investment,* helping you *effectively integrate a business operating system that fosters prioritization, communication, and collaboration.*** We focus on setting and achieving structured **goals** across various time-frames—from 90 days to ten years—with the core practice of weekly opportunity and obstacle meetings. These

INTRODUCTION

address operational challenges, enhance accountability, and create a forum for open feedback and strategic adjustments. The result? *A more efficient operations flow, a stronger team spirit, and significant financial growth—potentially adding substantial value to your business over time.*

As AI and new business operating systems continue to evolve, integrating these advancements will be critical. Clients will notice *and prefer businesses that adapt quickly, securing your competitive edge.* Profit remains vital, as it supports staff, enables equipment upgrades, and enhances client satisfaction. By involving your team in understanding key financial metrics, you'll drive meaningful engagement, accountability, and a shared vision of success.

About Me: A Journey of Leadership and Growth

With a background as both an **investment banker and business coach,** I offer a unique perspective. Over the past 30 years, I've assisted businesses in navigating issues related to finance, leadership, accountability, and culture. My comprehensive approach ensures a focus on **achieving the best return on investment, balancing time and resources wisely;** *while guiding individuals to work they love, alongside people they respect, with an inspiring plan & purpose.*

This book distills decades of financial and leadership knowledge into actionable steps. My philosophy is: "**We don't win or lose; we win or learn.**"

My passion has always been maximizing performance within business frameworks. I assist in aligning natural strengths with roles individuals love and excel in. Returning to college in 2005, I earned a **Master's in Transformational Leadership** from Bethel College. This program, inspired by Bill George, CEO of Medtronic, emphasized emotional intelligence for leadership, advocating vulnerability to foster collaboration, creativity, and excellence. It also exposed us to the power of a business operating systems that allow us to maximize the potential of the people that work with us and the business we were in.

I've helped business owners from all types of industries, Banking, pharmaceutical, manufacturing, law firms, investment banks, private equity companies, financial services, veterinary, dental, medical, commercial painting, etc..Every one of them made wise investment decisions for their businesses that could help their top line revenue expand and profits surge. I literally helped clients grow their PROFIT by 1000%, ie; $600,000 to $6,000,000. And that $6mm comes in year after year after year! This book offers you the *tools to maximize your business's potential, ensuring it thrives through inevitable changes*. Join me as we explore **strategies for collaboration, strategic planning, and culture building, poised to unleash your business's fullest potential.**

1

Embracing the Future, AI & Business operating systems overview

In an era of rapid technological advancement, embracing the future of business best practices, especially through AI readiness, is crucial. **AI integration marks a significant technological evolution**, and businesses must adapt quickly to harness its potential. They must also understand and integrate a business operating system because the 2 work in synergy together. One without the other and you will only harness maybe 1/3 of what AI can bring.

Understanding Business Operating Systems

As Tom Bouwer articulates in "What the Heck is EOS?", **every business relies on some form of operating system**, though it often remains undefined. A critical challenge is that many companies struggle to understand or implement the system effectively because **leadership teams lack consistency in applying disciplined processes.**

Consequences of Inconsistency:

Poor Communication: Inconsistent application of the operating system leads to breakdowns in communication, resulting in misunderstandings.

Dysfunction: Without a uniform approach, businesses often face operational dysfunction, making it difficult for teams to work cohesively.

Frustration and Confusion: Employees become frustrated and confused about priorities, as there is no consistent framework to guide their actions.

Unrealized Potential: Ultimately, the business fails to achieve its full potential due to these alignment issues.

The Good News:

Effective operating systems such as EOS, Pinnacle, and Bloom Growth have emerged, offering structured methodologies that enhance clarity and team alignment. By implementing these systems, practices align resources and strategies, steering towards success. Over 120,000 small businesses have excelled by integrating such systems, highlighting their transformative potential.

Maximizing Potential:

Adopting a structured operating system can vastly improve the functionality of a small business. By leveraging these frameworks, practices position themselves to efficiently integrate AI advancements and thrive amidst rapid technological change.

The Dawn of AI in Business application

Revolutionizing medical Practices. Fortunately, we are only in the 3rd inning rounding into the 4th with AI and many businesses stand poised to reap great benefits!

AI is increasingly integral to veterinary medicine, transforming patient care and management through:

Enhanced Diagnostics: AI offers rapid, accurate interpretations of X-rays and MRIs, aiding quick and precise veterinary diagnoses.

Predictive Health Monitoring: AI analyzes health data patterns for disease prediction, enabling proactive health interventions.

Telemedicine: AI-facilitated telemedicine expands medical,veteri-

nary care access, particularly in underserved areas.
Operational Efficiency: Automating routine administrative tasks like scheduling and billing, AI frees vets to focus on patient care.

Business optimization from AI

Customer Service: AI-powered chatbots and virtual assistants can handle customer queries around the clock, improving response times and customer satisfaction.

Data Analysis: AI can analyze large datasets quickly and accurately, uncovering insights and patterns that would be difficult for humans to detect.

Personalization: Businesses can use AI to deliver personalized experiences to customers, tailoring products, services, and marketing efforts to individual preferences and behaviors.

Predictive Analytics: AI helps in forecasting trends, customer behavior, and potential risks, enabling businesses to make informed decisions and stay ahead of the competition.

Automated Marketing: AI tools can automate marketing processes such as email campaigns, ad targeting, and social media management to optimize engagement and conversion rates.

Supply Chain Optimization: AI can revolutionize supply chain management by predicting demand, optimizing inventory, and reducing waste, thereby enhancing efficiency and cost-effectiveness.

Human Resources: AI can streamline the recruitment process by screening resumes and predicting candidate success, thus saving time and resources.

Fraud Detection: AI systems can detect fraudulent activities by analyzing transaction patterns and identifying anomalies in real-time.

These applications not only enhance operational efficiency but also provide a competitive edge by fostering innovation and improving customer experiences.

To fully benefit, businesses must maintain a structured system to integrate these technological innovations effectively.

Importance of a Certified Business Operating System: Operating systems like EOS, Pinnacle, Bloom Growth or a customized system built for your practice by a professional coach with expertise here, provide essential consistency, helping teams overcome common pitfalls:

Clarity and Alignment: Consistency in vision and goals ensures alignment across the team.

Improved Communication: Standardized communication practices minimize confusion and enhance team cohesiveness.

Structured Problem-Solving: A systematic framework for addressing issues supports continuous improvement.

Team Health and Morale: Clarified roles and direction boost team morale and support strategic growth.

By adopting such systems, you can fully exploit AI's potential, translating advancements into enhanced patient care, improved operations, better customer service and sustained growth.

Actionable Steps and Projected ROI:

1.Implement AI Tools:

Action: There are some recent AI applications that are already enhancing businesses substantially. For now, simply equip staff with the AI app like Chat GPT to explore AI's role in their tasks. Let your staff ask Chat some simple questions, like "I am a customer service rep in a medical practice, Do you have some ideas that can help me be more efficient?" I asked ChatGPT that question, and it gave 7 things you could do right away and specific strategies to implement. Let each department ask ChatGPT questions and simply have a meeting to hear all the new ideas they came up with! There you will find some low hanging fruit that can be installed instantly and reap immediate returns! The neat thing about AI, it really wants to help!

Projected ROI: Implementing these simple AI suggestions can save a small business owner approximately $20k to $50k annually through efficiency improvements, other more advanced applications substantially more!

2. Engage a Business Coach:

Action: Seek out a coach experienced with EOS, Bloom Growth, or Pinnacle to drive strategic practice improvements and financial acumen. A good coach will ask you good questions to foster big picture thinking on potential for your business. I've utilized and installed all 3 of the above systems.

Projected ROI: An experienced coach can potentially add $$$millions to business value over its life cycle by enhancing strategic thinking, sales, finance, culture and operations.

3. Evaluate your business attractiveness:

Action: Reflect on your small business's market readiness. Consider its turnkey nature and potential attractiveness to buyers. A good business coach will have a good process to evaluate your business's valuation and tips to add value.

Projected ROI: Enhancing business attractiveness can significantly increase its market value by 20% to 50%. More on this in an upcoming chapter.

These steps can free up time, increase revenue, or add more enjoyment to your life. They allow business owners to make more informed, impactful decisions. These actions help businesses not only adapt but also thrive in a rapidly evolving technological landscape.

2

Leading The Millennial Wave, Continuous Growth, Accountability = Essential Leadership Pillars

Millennials, typically defined as those born between 1981 and 1996, bring a unique set of strengths to the workplace, influenced by the era in which they grew up. Here are some key attributes that research and studies have identified, making millennials great workers:

1. **Tech-Savvy**: Growing up in an age of rapid technological advances, millennials naturally gravitate towards digital solutions and are adept at using technology to improve efficiency and productivity in the workplace.
2. **Value-Driven**: This generation places a high value on working for companies with missions and values that align with their own. They seek roles that provide purpose and meaning, leading to high levels of engagement when these align.
3. **Collaborative Nature**: Millennials thrive in team-oriented environments. They prefer open communication and collaboration, often resulting in innovative solutions and improved team dynam-

ics.
4. **Adaptability**: Raised during times of significant change, millennials are generally adaptable and open to new experiences. They are comfortable with change and can handle transitions such as shifts in workplace practices or technology.
5. **Continuous Learning**: Millennials value personal growth and are eager for opportunities to develop professionally. They seek ongoing education and training, which often results in a highly skilled and evolving workforce.
6. **Work-Life Balance**: While they value hard work, millennials also prioritize a healthy work-life balance. This perspective can lead to more sustainable productivity and can help prevent burnout.
7. **Diversity and Inclusion Champions**: Millennials tend to be more open-minded and supportive of diversity and inclusion in the workplace. They strive for workplaces that are equitable and inclusive, which can foster a more harmonious and productive work environment.

These attributes demonstrate why millennials, and next gens can be exceptional contributors to any organization. Their unique approach to work prioritizes efficiency, meaning, and balance, resulting in innovative and dynamic teams. Leveraging these strengths can lead to positive outcomes for both businesses and employees alike.

Here are real-world examples that help illustrate how millennials and next gen staff excel in the workplace with their unique attributes:
1. **Tech-Savvy**:
o **Example**: At companies like Facebook and Google, millennials lead in developing and employing cutting-edge technologies and innovations. Their familiarity with digital tools and platforms allows them to streamline processes and enhance productivity.
o **Impact**: Their ability to adapt quickly to new technologies means

they can efficiently manage remote work tools, which became crucial during the COVID-19 pandemic for maintaining business operations.

2. **Value-Driven**:

o **Example**: Companies such as Patagonia and Ben & Jerry's attract millennial workers with their focus on sustainability and social responsibility. These brands align their business operations with environmental and social values, which resonates deeply with millennial employees.

o **Impact**: This alignment can result in increased employee satisfaction and retention, as workers feel their personal values are supported by their employer.

3. **Collaborative Nature**:

o **Example**: At tech companies like Slack, the emphasis on teamwork and communication tools reflects the millennial penchant for collaboration. These environments are designed to foster open communication and teamwork, allowing for more creative problem-solving.

o **Impact**: Millennials' preference for collaboration often leads to a more inclusive approach to projects, gathering diverse perspectives that can drive innovation.

4. **Adaptability**:

o **Example**: Startups and fast-paced industries like fintech benefit from millennials' adaptability. Companies such as Square have thrived by leveraging young employees who can quickly adjust to industry disruptions and market changes.

o **Impact**: Their flexibility and readiness to embrace change help companies remain competitive and responsive to evolving business landscapes.

5. **Continuous Learning**:

o **Example**: LinkedIn provides extensive learning resources and encourages ongoing professional development, appealing to millennials' desire for growth. This dedication to constant learning helps employees keep skills up to date.

o **Impact**: Companies that support continuous learning see improvements in employee performance and innovation, as millennials bring fresh skills and ideas to the table.

6. **Work-Life Balance**:

o **Example**: Organizations like Dropbox have instituted flexible working hours and remote work policies, which appeal to millennials who seek work-life balance. This approach helps cater to their preference for balancing personal and professional commitments.

o **Impact**: By advocating for a balanced lifestyle, these companies often experience lower turnover rates and higher job satisfaction among employees.

7. **Diversity and Inclusion Champions**:

o **Example**: Salesforce and Microsoft are known for their strong diversity and inclusion initiatives, which attract millennials. These companies actively promote varied perspectives and backgrounds within their workforce.

o **Impact**: Millennials help foster work environments that prioritize inclusivity, leading to enhanced creativity and a wider array of innovative solutions.

By integrating these attributes and examples, organizations can harness the strengths of millennial workers to foster an agile, value-driven, and inclusive workplace that encourages growth and adaptability.

Embracing the values that millennials prioritize and **fostering a culture of continuous learning and innovative management techniques can yield significant benefits for employers. Here are some key advantages:**

1. **Enhanced Innovation and Creativity**:

o By supporting continuous learning and diverse management techniques, companies can tap into millennials' creative potential. These employees are likely to bring fresh perspectives and innovative solutions to business challenges.

2. **Increased Employee Engagement and Retention**:
o Aligning company values with those of millennial employees fosters a sense of purpose and belonging. Engaged employees are more committed and less likely to leave, reducing turnover rates and the associated costs of hiring and training new staff.

3. **Agile and Adaptable Workforce**:
o Encouraging constant development ensures that the workforce remains agile and responsive to market changes. This adaptability is crucial for companies operating in fast-paced industries where innovation dictates success.

4. **Improved Organizational Culture**:
o Emphasizing values such as work-life balance, inclusivity, and continuous growth helps create a positive organizational culture. Such environments attract top talent and facilitate a collaborative atmosphere where all employees can thrive.

5. **Stronger Brand Reputation**:
o Companies that embody progressive and inclusive practices build a strong brand reputation. This public image can attract more customers, partners, and top-notch talent, further enhancing the company's competitive edge.

6. **Better Problem-Solving and Decision-Making**:
o A workforce that is continuously learning brings new skills and perspectives to the table. This diversity of thought leads to better problem-solving strategies and more informed decision-making processes.

7. **Increased Productivity and Efficiency**:
o Engaged employees who are continually learning and applying new techniques are generally more productive. They contribute to more efficient workflows and processes, thereby improving the overall performance of the organization.

8. **Alignment with Future Trends**:
o By adopting values aligned with millennial priorities, companies

position themselves to seamlessly integrate future workplace trends, maintaining relevance and competitiveness in an ever-evolving market. By leveraging these benefits, employers not only **secure the loyalty and productivity of their millennial workforce but also enhance their overall business performance** and sustainability. This win-win scenario ensures that both employees and employers thrive in a dynamic and challenging business environment.

Investing in the career development of millennial staff can lead to several monetary benefits for organizations. Here are some of the financial advantages:

1. **Reduced Turnover Costs**:

o High employee turnover is costly, factoring in recruitment, training, and lost productivity. By fostering career development, companies can enhance employee satisfaction and loyalty, significantly reducing turnover rates and the associated costs.

2. **Increased Productivity and Efficiency**:

o Career development programs equip employees with new skills and knowledge, leading to improved productivity and efficiency. This increase in workplace efficiency can have a direct positive impact on the company's bottom line.

3. **Higher Employee Engagement**:

o Engaged employees often perform better, contributing to higher revenue per employee. Career development opportunities can boost engagement levels, translating to increased performance and profitability.

4. **Innovation and Competitive Edge**:

o By encouraging learning and development, companies often spur innovation. Employees who are skilled and knowledgeable will drive innovative projects that can open new revenue streams and provide a competitive advantage in the market.

5. **Enhanced Reputation and Attraction of Talent**:

o Companies known for investing in employee development often attract top talent, reducing recruitment costs. A strong reputation as a learning organization can negate the need for expensive recruitment drives and increase the quality of applicants.

6. **Better Customer Service and Satisfaction**:

o Well-developed employees tend to deliver superior customer service, enhancing customer satisfaction and loyalty. Happy customers are more likely to return and recommend the business, leading to increased sales.

7. **Efficiency in Adapting to Market Changes**:

o Skilled employees can quickly adapt to new technologies and processes, minimizing downtime and retraining costs. This agility enables businesses to respond swiftly to market demands, maintaining or increasing market share.

8. **Cultivation of Future Leaders**:

o Investing in talent development helps identify and prepare future leaders within the organization, reducing the need for costly external hires. Promoting internally can save on recruitment and on-boarding costs, while also retaining valuable organizational knowledge.

By focusing on your next gens career development, companies not only foster a more engaged and productive workforce but also realize tangible financial benefits that contribute to long-term business success.

What role does accountability play in promoting a healthy culture and fostering career growth in our next gen employees?

Accountability plays a crucial role in fostering a healthy organizational culture and supporting career growth, especially for next-generation employees like millennials and Gen Z. Here's **how accountability contributes** to these aspects:

1. **Enhances Trust and Transparency**:

o When accountability is ingrained in the culture, it fosters a transparent environment where employees trust leadership and each other.

This transparency builds a strong foundation for open communication, crucial for a healthy workplace culture.

2. **Empowers Employees**:
o *By holding employees accountable, organizations empower them to take ownership of their roles and responsibilities.* This empowerment leads to increased confidence and encourages proactive contributions, which aids in personal and professional growth.

3. **Drives Performance**:
o Accountability *ensures that employees are aware of their goals and how their actions impact the organization. This awareness motivates them to perform better* and strive for excellence, which can lead to career advancements.

4. **Encourages Responsibility**:
o When employees know they are accountable for their outcomes, they are *more likely to act responsibly and make informed decisions. This sense of responsibility promotes maturity and professional development.*

5. **Facilitates Feedback and Improvement**:
o Regularly assessing performance and holding individuals accountable allows for *constructive feedback. This feedback is essential for individual growth as it highlights areas of improvement and encourages ongoing learning.*

6. **Promotes Teamwork and Collaboration**:
o Accountability in team settings **enhances collaboration as team members** rely on each other to meet shared objectives. This strengthens teamwork and builds a supportive environment conducive to collective and individual success.

7. **Aligns Personal and Organizational Goals**:
o Holding employees accountable a*ligns their personal career progression with organizational objectives, creating a win-win situation.* Employees are more motivated to achieve their personal goals when they see how they contribute to the organization's success.

8. **Encourages Goal Setting**:

o Accountability encourages clear *goal setting, both personally and professionally. By setting and evaluating goals, employees can track their progress and take ownership of their career paths, while also driving company success.*

Incorporating a culture of accountability nurtures an environment where next-gen employees can thrive and develop their careers. It ensures that individuals feel valued and challenged, which helps in retaining talented employees and building a strong, dynamic workforce.

Financial Implications:

- **Initial Costs**: Investment in technology and employee training will be the most immediate financial requirements. However, these should be viewed as strategic investments that enhance operational efficiency and service quality.
- **Long-term Savings**: Improved employee retention and productivity will lead to significant cost savings. Enhanced operational efficiency can reduce overtime and eliminate redundant tasks.
- **Revenue Growth**: By offering superior service and maintaining high client satisfaction, your practice can increase client retention and attract new clients through referrals.
- **Competitive Edge**: *Practices that embrace these principles may find additional revenue streams as they attract clientele seeking cutting-edge veterinary care distinguished by excellent service and personal attention.*

In summary, understand that Next Gens need to be challenged and be in a career growth, business growth environment or they get restless and look for the next challenge. Implementing these strategies requires thoughtful investment, but **the long-term gains in efficiency, employee satisfaction, and client loyalty can offset these costs, ultimately benefiting the financial health of your business.**

3

Deeper Dive, Leveraging Operating Systems with AI, Maximum Benefit

OK, quick point to make here. I am a member of the Baby boomer generation. I may not be the brightest bulb in the closet when it comes to technology, but I do have a certain amount of common sense. I've seen enough technological advances to realize this one is going to be a good one. It will make life easier for a lot of people. Probably, the key point to understand is your customers are using AI. In April of this year the Chat GPT app had nearly 2 billion visits. So, our customers will start expecting businesses to have it. The first adopters will have an advantage. This is one of those movements that is going to make us adapt quickly or we will have to understand we could lose business to those that have already adapted.

AI has become increasingly accessible to small businesses, offering tools that can enhance efficiency and customer experiences across various industries. Here are some practical AI applications for small businesses in sectors like restaurants, accounting, medical, HR, and customer service:

1. **Restaurants:**

- **ChatGPT** for automated reservation handling and customer inquiries.
- **7shifts:** AI-powered employee scheduling to optimize staff hours and reduce labor costs.
- **PlateIQ:** Automates invoice processing and integrates with accounting systems.

1. **Accounting:**

- **QuickBooks Online:** Utilizes machine learning to categorize transactions automatically and provide insights on business performance.
- **Xero:** Provides AI-driven cash flow forecasting and analytics.

1. **Medical:**

- **Zebra Medical Vision:** Offers AI tools that assist radiologists by analyzing medical imaging for faster and more accurate diagnosis.
- **Buoy Health:** Provides an AI-powered health assistant that helps patients understand their symptoms and find appropriate care.

1. **Human Resources:**

- **Breezy HR:** AI recruitment software that streamlines the hiring process by automating repetitive tasks like resume screening and candidate communication.
- **Gusto:** Incorporates AI to manage payroll, benefits, and compliance efficiently.

1. **Customer Service:**

- **Zendesk:** Offers AI features such as Answer Bot to assist users and improve the customer support experience.
- **Freshdesk:** Leverages AI to automate responses to frequent queries and learn from interactions to better support customers.

These applications can significantly enhance how small businesses operate by saving time, reducing costs, and providing better service. They are typically scalable and affordable, making them an excellent fit for smaller operations.

Here are the benefits to a business from having an **up-to-date technology with the human side of the business, meaning a system for organizing our human energy,** combined with the potential that AI is offering. *So here is the **key point** I believe I am driving home here.* I hope so. The human side of the business is very special and precious. Hopefully we do not have a future that is all robots and AI. Our fellow workers are key. Yes, we all have flaws, but it is in the cooperation, the teamwork, collaboration, the team planning, building purpose and values into the business, the prioritizing, the roles clarification, leading and managing, the day to day living and working together is where the beauty lies! This is what a good operating system helps you and your team accomplish.

It is through these types of tools and good coaching, that **we are shaped and molded into better people.** Better friends, better teammates, better spouses, better parents. This is the beauty of teams! Good teams shape us and mold us into better versions of ourselves. They are truly a blessing to the people that work there and the clientele they serve. We do not have enough of these types of businesses in the world. **A good coach, good owners, team leaders, along with these 2 technologies have the potential to make an incredible impact on** your team and their communities! Integrating AI tools with your *"Business Operating System"* like Traction, Bloom Growth or Pinnacle can create a **powerful synergy.** Let's look at an example from the veterinary space, that enhances efficiency, patient care, cost savings, and revenue. I worked with a Vet group that 10x'd their business with this operating system. Here's how they can work together:

Synergistic Benefits

1. Enhanced Operational Efficiency

- **BOS Framework**: Provides a structured approach to organizing the business practice, with defined roles, clear goals, and accountability processes. This creates a more disciplined approach to managing tasks and meeting objectives.
- **AI Automation**: Handles repetitive tasks such as scheduling, reminders, and patient follow-ups, reducing the workload on staff and minimizing human error. This allows the team to focus on strategic and patient care activities outlined by your BOS.

2. Improved Patient Care

- **BOS Clarity**: Ensures that everyone is aligned with the practice's mission and patient care goals, enhancing teamwork and patient interaction.
- **AI Diagnostics and Monitoring**: Uses advanced analytics to improve accuracy and speed of diagnoses, providing better outcomes for patients. AI can also monitor patient data continuously, alerting staff to issues proactively.

3. Cost Savings

- **BOS Financial Management**: Offers systems for tracking financial metrics closely, identifying inefficiencies, and ensuring optimal resource allocation.
- **AI Cost Efficiency**: Reduces operational costs by streamlining processes, improving inventory management, and reducing diagnostic errors—all of which contribute to financial savings.

4. Increased Revenue

- **BOS Growth Strategies**: Establishes clear pathways for growth, keeping the team focused on expanding services and improving client retention.
- **AI Upselling and Cross-Selling**: Analyzes client data to identify opportunities for offering additional services or products, enhancing revenue per client.

Implementation Approach

1. **Strategic Planning**: Use BOS to define strategic objectives and incorporate AI tools to meet these objectives efficiently.
2. **Process Integration**: Implement AI solutions that align with your BOS-defined processes for scheduling, financial management, and client communication.
3. **Continuous Improvement**: Leverage AI analytics to provide insights and feedback on operations, allowing the BOS framework to adapt and refine processes for continuous improvement.
4. **Training and Culture**: Cultivate a culture of learning where staff understands both the BOS methodology and AI applications, encouraging innovation and agile responses to challenges.

By combining the strategic framework and discipline of BOS with the cutting-edge capabilities of AI, your business practice can operate more effectively, deliver superior client care, realize significant cost savings, and drive revenue growth, all while fostering a supportive and innovative workplace environment. ✨

The results of the synergistic combination of these 2 systems:

Integrating AI tools and an operating system like Bloom Growth can significantly *enhance the culture of a business practice by fostering a more empowered, efficient, and collaborative environment. Here's how* **solving problems faster** *can positively impact practice culture*:

1. Empowerment and Confidence

- **Rapid Problem-Solving**: When issues are resolved quickly, staff members feel more capable and empowered in their roles. This boost in confidence encourages them to take initiative and make proactive decisions.
- **Skill Development**: As staff engage with AI technologies and strategic frameworks, they acquire new skills and knowledge, which increases their sense of value and professional growth.

2. Collaboration and Teamwork

- **Aligned Goals**: BOS helps create a clear vision and shared goals, which unites the team around common objectives, improving collaboration.
- **Enhanced Communication**: With AI handling routine tasks and providing insights, team members have more time to communicate effectively and work collaboratively on complex issues.

3. Efficiency and Focus

- **Less Stress**: Automating routine tasks reduces workload pressure,

leading to less stress and a more positive work environment.
- **Focus on Value-adding Activities**: Freed from mundane tasks, staff can focus on higher-value activities, such as patient care or client interaction, which are more rewarding and fulfilling.

4. Innovation and Adaptability

- **Culture of Innovation**: Regular interaction with AI systems encourages a mindset of continuous improvement and learning, promoting an innovative culture.
- **Agility**: By solving problems faster, the practice becomes more adaptable to changes and challenges, making the team resilient and open to new opportunities.

5. Job Satisfaction and Retention

- **Increased Satisfaction**: A supportive culture that embraces efficient problem-solving reduces frustration and boosts job satisfaction.
- **Higher Retention Rates**: Happy and engaged employees are more likely to stay, reducing turnover and fostering long-term team cohesion.

By streamlining problem-solving and enhancing operational efficiencies, AI and a strong operating system, together, contribute to a positive, innovative, and adaptable workplace culture. This not only improves daily operations but also elevates overall job satisfaction, making the business a more attractive place to work for current and future staff members. ☆You are probably starting to see how this combination of systems can exponentially advance a practice's morale, profits and fun. Give me a call so we can

discuss installing a program like this into your practice. (847)-372-3432.

Let me say something here that I believe you need to be aware of. A good coach educating the operating system into the team's daily work routines, installing the habitual disciplines of the core processes of the operating system, the system pays for itself! Nine times out of ten the ROI is considerably higher. I Installed these operating systems into companies that had 3x, 5x, 10x returns on the original investment! Let me also make something else abundantly clear. After the system is installed and the coach walks away from the install part of the transaction, the company continues to reap the benefits of the installed operating system that maximizes the human capital in your business. You get to reap the benefits of those extra profits for years to come!

The combination of these 2 technologies will be very rewarding to the businesses that take action!

4

A-Players, Developing and Retaining Talent

"*Sometimes it's easier to change people than to change the people.*"
- Greg Cleary

"To significantly increase your revenue and profit, start by elevating your leadership team."

You might not always recognize if you have the wrong people on your team. They may seem suitable until you bring in a few A-players, and the difference becomes evident. These A-players might not have the most industry experience or the perfect academic background, but their presence is transformative. For example, one client's company experienced unprecedented growth with a new team, allowing the owner to enjoy family vacations, even during peak seasons. This transformation was sparked by creating a cohesive leadership team of A-players. Focusing on securing A-players can be a game-changer. Assess your leadership team: Who might be in the wrong seat?

Empower A-Players
Once you hire A-players, allow them the freedom to excel. Provide

them with ample space to lead, and they will tackle significant challenges and drive success. Generously investing in them is crucial, as the ROI of an A-player is consistently worthwhile. Their impact is immediate, often beginning on day one.

Nurturing and Retaining A-Players

Adopt structured approaches inspired by leadership and talent management strategies to develop and retain A-players. Here's how:

1. **Develop A-Players:**

   o **Talent Identification**: Regularly evaluate performance to identify those with high potential who exceed expectations and exhibit leadership qualities.

   o **Personal Development Plans**: Customize development plans to enhance individual strengths and align with their career aspirations, offering avenues for skill development and leadership roles.

2. **Provide Growth Opportunities:**

   o **Mentorship and Coaching**: Establish mentorship programs for A-players to exchange roles as mentors and mentees, facilitating learning and leadership.

   o **Challenging Assignments**: Give projects that challenge their abilities, encouraging innovation and skill demonstration.

3. **Recognition and Rewards:**

   o **Public Acknowledgment**: Regularly recognize their contributions in meetings or newsletters, ensuring they feel valued and seen.

   o **Performance-Based Incentives**: Offer bonuses, promotions, or special opportunities to motivate continuous excellence.

This is key: "Understanding A-Player Needs":
1. **Feedback and Involvement**:
o Regularly provide feedback and involve A-players in strategic discussions to align their goals with the organization's goals.
2. **Career Advancement**:
o Clearly outline career paths and provide leadership development programs to prepare them for higher responsibilities.
3. **Work-Life Balance**:
o Offer flexible work arrangements, ensuring a healthy work-life balance which is crucial for engagement.
4. **Impactful Work**:
o Ensure roles have a clear purpose and impact, making their work more meaningful and satisfying.

By strategically developing and addressing the needs of A-players, Businesses can cultivate an environment where talent thrives and contributes their best efforts to the organization's success. Additionally, for engaging young talent, focus on promoting a dynamic and inclusive culture while ensuring meaningful, flexible work experiences.

Here are *three action steps and examples of potential returns on investment, time, and cultural contributions* when focusing on nurturing, attracting, and retaining A-Players in your veterinary practice:

Action Steps
1. **Conduct Regular Talent Audits:**
o Evaluate your team regularly to identify high-potential employees. Use performance metrics and leadership assessments to ensure you have the right people in the right roles.
2. **Implement a Comprehensive Mentorship Program:**
o Establish programs that pair A-players with both new hires and seasoned employees. This can help share knowledge, encourage leadership development, and foster a learning culture within your

practice.

3. **Offer Competitive Compensation and Flexible Work Arrangements:**
   o Ensure your compensation packages are competitive and align with industry standards. Additionally, provide options for flexible work hours or remote work, which can increase job satisfaction and retain top talent.

Potential ROI Examples

1. **Return on Investment (ROI):**
   o By investing in high-quality professional development and leadership training, you can reduce turnover and lower the costs associated with hiring and training new employees. High-performing A-players can boost revenue growth through enhanced client service and innovation in practice operations.

2. **Return on Time:**
   o A cohesive team of A-players can streamline processes, enhance efficiency, and reduce the time spent on problem-solving. This allows you to focus on strategic business initiatives rather than day-to-day operational challenges.

3. **Return on Culture:**
   o Cultivating a team of A-players can enhance your practice's culture by fostering an environment of excellence, collaboration, and innovation. This positive culture not only attracts top talent but also improves client satisfaction and loyalty, as employees are more engaged and motivated.

   o **Implementing these strategies can significantly impact your business practice success, providing tangible benefits in terms of financial performance, operational efficiency, and organizational culture.**

5

The Power of a "Next Gen Engaged Culture" and How to Get It

Lena, the leader of a bustling veterinary hospital, was known for her kindness, patience, and big heart. Her vision was clear: to embed the Big Three deliverables—Security, Connection and Purpose, —within her hospital staff. With a strong desire to foster a nurturing environment, Lena sought to transform the hospital's culture and aligned with a coaching process to achieve this.

Coaching Process:

Together, we embarked on a journey to instill **a disciplined meeting cadence, crucial to cultivating a strong, healthy culture.** Our approach emphasized creating a **safe, collaborative space where team members could openly share obstacles and opportunities, achieving growth both individually and collectively.**

A key component of this transformation was **taking the leadership team away for two, one-day retreat sessions.** These retreats provided the necessary environment for deep reflection and strategic planning, where **the leadership team of the hospital discerned and committed to live by values that resonated deeply with their mission: Teamwork, Passion for Excellence, Compassionate Care,** and Trusted Partnerships. These values became the foundation for their culture. They also collaborated on their long-term vision and goals for the hospital. This new Vision, Goals and Values guided all subsequent decisions and actions.

Here is the structure of the staff meetings used to *assure accountability to goals.*

The meeting cadence included:

- **Daily Huddles (10 minutes):** Quick check-ins to address immediate issues, what we learned yesterday and align today's priorities.
- **Weekly Opportunities & Obstacles Meeting (60 minutes):** This pivotal meeting accelerates efficiency by addressing hurdles and seizing new opportunities, fostering fluidity, joy, and growth.

Meeting Structure:

1. **Check-in (5 minutes):** Team members share recent positive experiences, fostering a positive atmosphere.
2. **90-Day Goal Progress (5 minutes):** Updates on quarterly goals ensure accountability, moving unresolved challenges to the Obstacle and Opportunity (O/O) box for solution.
3. **Weekly Data Points or KPIs (5 minutes):** Reviewing key metrics allows the team to gauge progress and impact.
4. **Headlines (5 minutes):** Share important updates, both for the team and clients, ensuring awareness and engagement.
5. **To-Dos Completion (5 minutes):** Accountability checks for assigned tasks, reinforcing commitment to actions.
6. **Obstacles and Opportunities (30 minutes):** Focused discussion for resolving challenges and integrating new opportunities, with

actionable to-dos.
7. **Wrap-up (5 minutes):** Summarize key messages for broader staff communication and rate the meeting to ensure effectiveness and alignment.

- **Quarterly All-Day Meeting (8 hours):** Off-site comprehensive reviews of the annual plan, revisiting values, evaluating plans, celebrating wins, learning from mistakes, and setting 90-day priorities.

Action Steps:

1. **Implement the Meeting Cadence:** Begin with establishing the daily and weekly meetings to foster a consistent rhythm and habit of accountability.
2. **Define Key Performance Indicators (KPIs):** Identify and agree on the critical metrics that align with growth and quality service goals.
3. **Assign and Track 90-Day Goals:** Clearly assign objectives linked to these KPIs and ensure regular progress checks.

Results and Benefits:
As the leadership team came together, they d**iscovered a shared ambition: to expand their 24/7/365 care into communities lacking life-saving veterinary services.** This breakthrough **underscored a universal truth—everyone has a need to grow and become the best version of themselves.** The team realized that career development pathways are vital, particularly for younger generations, who often seek continual growth and avoid roles that feel stagnating.

In today's rapidly evolving business landscape, veterinary managers and practice owners must recognize that change, accelerated by the internet and AI, is inevitable. The **younger staff, those under 40, closely observe whether businesses are keeping pace with these changes. If not, they are likely to move to more innovative and forward-thinking environments. This shift is also evident among customers who are increasingly adopting AI to enhance their lives.**

With this robust framework in place, Lena and her team not only cultivated a vibrant and accountable culture but also achieved remarkable success. Over four years, **the hospital experienced a remarkable 300% growth**, establishing itself as the premier 24/7 pet hospital in the area.

ROI Benefits:

1. **Increased Efficiency:** The streamlined meetings and clear action steps enabled the team to address challenges swiftly, enhancing overall productivity.
2. **High Employee Retention:** By creating clear growth pathways and ensuring team engagement, the hospital retained skilled professionals who were committed to the mission.
3. **Enhanced Client Satisfaction:** The focus on critical KPIs and seamless teamwork translated into improved client service and satisfaction, contributing to the hospital's reputation and growth.
4. **The power of these strategic retreats:** and disciplined processes showcased how a committed leadership team, supported by **shared values and a clear mission, can drive cultural transformation and achieve significant success.**

Further Reading:

For anyone interested in deepening their understanding of building a strong culture tailored for modern generations, I highly recommend *"The Culture Code"* by Daniel Coyle. This book provides valuable

THE POWER OF A "NEXT GEN ENGAGED CULTURE" AND HOW TO GET IT

insights into the elements that make a successful team culture, offering practical ideas that can be applied to any organizational setting.

I also recommend "**What the Heck is EOS**" by Gino Wickman and Tom Bauer, as well as "***Pinnacle: Five Principles that take Your Business to the Top of the Mountain***." By Greg Cleary and Steve Preda. These 2 cover operating systems, A-Players, meeting cadence.

6

Leveraging Good Coaching for Enhanced Performance

Coaching and mentorship play a vital role in professional development and can significantly contribute to creating an impactful workplace culture. Here's what you need to consider about this topic:

The Role of Coaching and Mentorship
1. Empowerment Through Guidance:

- Coaching and mentorship are powerful tools for empowering individuals. They provide a platform for sharing knowledge and skills, **helping people unlock their potential and become more confident in their abilities.**

2. Creating Safe Spaces:

- Establishing an environment where employees feel safe to express themselves is crucial. These spaces allow individuals to be vulnerable, honest, and transparent, leading to genuine communication and deeper connections.

3. Encouraging Vulnerability and Transparency:

- Vulnerability is no longer seen as a weakness but rather a strength in today's evolving workplaces. It encourages open dialogue, fosters trust, and enables team members to provide and receive constructive feedback.

4. The Demand from Next-Gen Employees:

- The next generation highly values workplaces where they feel understood and supported. They look for mentors and coaches who can offer structured guidance while valuing transparency and collaborative feedback.

A Future Focused on Support: The **demand for supportive mentorship is particularly strong among the next generation of employees. They seek guidance and clarity, looking for mentors who can not only guide them in their careers** but also help them navigate their personal aspirations.

Now here is how I coach your leaders and managers to implement this.

1. **Leverage the Right Roles:**

o Ensure that the **right people are in the right seat**s within your organization. This involves assessing employees' strengths and aligning them with their roles to maximize productivity and satisfaction. I also use the Gallup organizations Strength Finder online talent assessment.

o https://www.gallup.com/cliftonstrengths/en/252137/home.aspx

o This test helps your employee, and you see what their natural born strengths are. This way you can help guide them into **their best area to succeed and make their greatest contribution** to your business.

2. **Clear Accountability:**

o Establish **clear responsibility lines** so everyone knows their duties and accountability. This promotes **ownership and efficient workflow management** in the team.

3. **Provide Regular Feedback:**

o Engage in consistent feedback loops with your team. Communication should be open, honest, and frequent to motivate employees and help them grow. Feedback is the breakfast of champions!

o I recommend a 90 day "1 on 1" with each employee. A good book for using that format is *"How to Be a Great Boss"* by Gino Wickman

4. **Foster Strong Relationships:**

o Build genuine relationships with your team members. Understanding them on a personal level strengthens mutual respect and collaboration.

5. **Use Data for Effective Management:**

o Implement metrics and KPIs as part of data-driven management to objectively measure performance and make informed decisions.

o They want to know how well they are doing. A good **scorecard and talent assessment tools** art great for creating awareness and guidance for improvement.

6. **Lead by Example:**

o Demonstrate the behavior and work ethic you expect from your team. Leading by example inspires employees and sets the standard for the organization. **During 1/1 time ask each employee how they think you are doing? What do they see that could help you do better?**

These principles are designed to help supervisors *create a productive and positive workplace culture, helping both the business and the employees to excel.*

Some companies and sports teams that lead the field with coaching and mentoring and are worth mentioning here:

San Antonio Spurs (NBA):

LEVERAGING GOOD COACHING FOR ENHANCED PERFORMANCE

- The Spurs are known for their strong culture built on trust, transparency, and mutual respect. Coach Gregg Popovich emphasizes personal relationships and open communication, nurturing an environment where players feel valued and understood.

Salesforce:

- Salesforce promotes a culture of feedback through mentorship. Their V2MOM process (Vision, Values, Methods, Obstacles, and Measures) helps employees align personal and professional goals while fostering transparent communication throughout all levels of the organization.

Let's commit to creating an environment where coaching and mentorship become integral to your team culture. By doing so, you will not only achieve your collective goals but also empower each other to reach new heights of personal and professional excellence.

7

Assessing Your Business's Value in the Eyes of Investors

In the realm of small business, businesses with 10-200 employees, understanding how to navigate private equity and investment is pivotal. This chapter will empower you to **confidently evaluate the value of your business and find the right private equity (PE) partner, ensuring your business's success and longevity.**

Understanding Your Business's Worth

Assessing your business value is a crucial step when potential buyers express interest. My background as an investment banker and my credentials in Transformational Leadership and Business Operating Systems equip me to guide you in this journey. Here's what we focus on:

Questions a good buyer will ask *and questions you need to know.*

1- Are you running on a certified operating system installed by a qualified coach? How far into the organization is the system? Is every employee aware of the system and in a weekly opportunity/obstacle meeting?

2- How many competitors are there in your market?

3- How unique is your business in the market? Is there a strong

competitive advantage?
4- How functional and aligned are your leadership team? Are all leaders open and honest? Are they willing to become their best?
5- Is the business growing? At what rate? 0-100?
6- What types of regulations are attached to the business?
7- How much debt do they have? Do they need a capital infusion and how much?
8- How aligned is the leadership team around culture? Healthy or Toxic?
These above questions with EBITDA determine your value.

Actionable Steps and Projected ROI

1. **Implement a Certified Business Operating System:**

o **Action:** Introduce a business operating system such as EOS, Pinnacle, Bloom Growth or a customized system designed for your team by a good, experienced coach. These streamline operations and maximize efficiency. Building a more turnkey practice. Also, a more liquid practice making it more attractive to potential investors/buyers.

o **Projected ROI:** A potential **increase in practice value by 25% to 100% within 12 to 18** months due to increased operational efficiency and marketability.

2. **Conduct a Comprehensive Market Analysis:**

o **Action:** Analyze the local market dynamics, including growth potential and competitive landscape.

o **Projected ROI:** A strategic understanding can position the business for a premium valuation, potentially increasing market value based on effective positioning and competitive differentiation.

3. **Engage Professional Guidance for Valuation:**

o **Action:** Work with financial and industry experts to accurately assess practice value and prepare for negotiations.

o **Projected ROI:** Secure a sale price 20% + above initial offers by understanding true market value and enhancing negotiation capability.

By taking these actions, you'll not only enhance the value of your practice but also ensure a smoother transition, greater financial return and produce a better list of options for you.

1. **Evaluate Options:**
o Decide whether to continue independently or partner with a PE investor.
2. **Plan Your Future:**
o Determine your retirement timeline.
o Decide whether you want to retire from practice.
o Consider enhancing your business by implementing a custom business operating system combined with advanced AI to boost team efficiency, profitability, and value. The timeline to adequately install an operating system is 18-24. So if you are thinking about retiring in the next 3-5 years the time to find your advocate to help your discern your best options is now.
3. **Reap the Benefits:**
o Gain flexibility in retirement, whether selling your practice for the best price or continuing to draw income while **working *on your terms.***

Deciphering EBITDA

Understanding EBITDA is key to evaluating your practice's market value. EBITDA—Earnings Before Interest, Taxes, Depreciation, and Amortization—offers a clear view of operational performance, vital for comparison and valuation:

- **Operational Efficiency:** Allows for comparison across companies by removing non-operating factors.
- **Valuation Tool:** Indicates potential cash flow, essential for mergers and acquisitions.
- **Limitations:** Does not address capital expenditures or debt.

Using EBITDA alongside other metrics (The 8 questions above) can provide a comprehensive financial analysis.

Ensuring a Fair Price and a Smooth Sale

To secure a good price and streamline the selling process, consider these strategies:

- **Seek Expert Guidance:** Partner with a knowledgeable mentor familiar with finance, valuations, and PE acquisitions.
- **Plan for Post-Sale:** Know what will happen to your practice and team post-purchase.
- **Understand Contracts:** Clarify responsibilities and the duration you're bound to the practice's success post-sale.

Identifying the Right PE Partner

Choosing the right PE partner is critical for your practice and employees. Here's what to expect:

- You may need to stay engaged for 1-2 years post-sale, ensuring a smooth transition.
- Be prepared for potential conflicts if your vision differs from that of the buyer.
- Understand the implications of changes imposed by the new owners.

To identify an ideal PE buyer, they should:

1. Be running on a certified business operating system like EOS, Pinnacle, or Bloom Growth.
2. Demonstrate market expertise and a commitment to sustainable growth by showcasing their track record.
3. Present a compelling vision, values, and mission that align with your practice ethos.

If the buyer cannot demonstrate alignment with these principles, reconsider the sale, and consult with me for buyers who value this informed process. It is key to understand what the buyer brings to the table that will benefit your team and improve their lives.

It's important that you understand the above so you can have confidence when talking to a potential buyer/investor. Most owners are not aware of how to value their practice so they can get the best results for themselves and their team. **Remember, your team will be working for the new owner.** Your best bet always is **keep asking, "How turnkey is my business? Can I go away for a month and the business still runs well, has high customer satisfaction and profit at 15-20%? Can problems be solved without me? Does my team collaborate well? What grade would I give our culture? Are we in synergy with AI & our Business Operating System? Know the answers to these questions and if your answers are no for some get to work!** Most buyers come along when the owner is unprepared. Don't let that be you.

Do you know the value of your business? Would you like to get to know specifically what your business is worth? I can help you with that. I work as a business owner advocate to help you with all the questions and challenges that come up in business. I can work with you and show you what the value of your business is with my practice valuation tools. **You can contact me, Mike Johnson at (847)-372-3432 or email me at askmj12@gmail.com.** I would be happy to help you.

8

Charting a Path to Future Success

I hope this little book has ignited a desire in you to embrace powerful, positive changes in your business in 2025! Your business isn't just a business; it's a platform to bring stability and security to your family, staff, and community. Remember, the Big Three—Security, Connection and Purpose—are what everyone seeks in their work today.

Embrace the seven systems and processes discussed in this book; **the potential rewards are significant, turning even a modest enterprise into a multi-million-dollar success story.** *Lena's journey exemplifies the profound impact of a strong culture and a committed team, driving growth and fulfillment.* Her team's dreams are realized not just within the practice, but as leaders and experts in their communities.

As you are aware, AI is advancing rapidly, offering both challenges and opportunities. Next-generation employees seek growth, mentorship, and coaching. Using potent operating systems like EOS, Pinnacle, Bloom Growth or a customized system built for your practice, they can greatly enhance your practice's efficiency and impact. *As a business coach, I've seen firsthand how these systems transform businesses, but the journey is difficult to navigate alone. This is where a coach's expertise becomes invaluable.*

We've also covered **how to evaluate and increase your business's value, particularly in the eyes of potential private equity buyers**. Understanding your enterprise value is crucial, not just for selling, but for ensuring it aligns with good business operating systems and secure partnerships.

My passion lies in working with a select few clients who are driven to build exceptional business practices for a greater purpose. The time to act is now. AI and modern business management tools await implementation, setting the stage for your accelerated success.

For those **ready to take the next step**, I am here to offer support, guidance, and coaching to help you navigate this exciting journey. **Contact me at askmj12@gmail.com or call 847-372-3432.** You can also see me on LinkedIn (Michael R Johnson, MATL). Let's move forward together, transforming your business for long-lasting impact and success.

9

Conclusion Story & Contact information

As we draw this journey to a close, **I'd like to share a story with you from an inspiring chapter in my own life.** In my early years, I had the privilege of playing football at **Illinois Valley Community College**, under the guidance of **coach Vince McMahon**, a man who **embodied leadership, passion, and purpose. His philosophy was simple yet profound: practice as you play, cherish every victory, and develop the character needed to pursue significant goals.**

Our team, bound by hard work and camaraderie, achieved something pretty special. We went undefeated, winning the Midwest Bowl and earning honors that echo decades later. But beyond trophies and accolades, **what Vince instilled in us went far deeper. He taught us the value of teamwork, respect, and excellence—a legacy that extends far beyond the playing field.**

In the business world, much like sports, success is forged through the power of a cohesive, purpose-driven team. Every business is a tapestry of diverse talents, courage and unique strengths. As leaders, our role is to cultivate an environment where each team member can thrive and contribute to a shared vision. **Through effective coaching, we empower individuals with the skills, mindset, and resilience needed to succeed not just professionally but in life.**

Just as Vince knew that every win was a steppingstone to building a family of future leaders and coaches, we too **must recognize that our businesses are fertile grounds for growing talents and fostering lifelong friendships. When a team operates in harmony, embracing complementary strengths, they create a culture of collaboration, courage, creativity, and continual growth.**

And, like my experience on that unforgettable team, **your business can offer employees a platform where work becomes more than a job—it becomes a calling filled with joy, challenge, and achievement.** By nurturing such a team dynamic, **you're not only sculpting future successes but also crafting a legacy of empowered individuals who will carry forward these teachings into broader aspects of life. Pause and think about that for a minute.**

Through inspired leadership, we can provide the same gifts Vince bestowed upon us: **cherished memories, enduring relationships, and the skills to help others win. A business led with purpose can change lives, one team member at a time. This is the ultimate testament to a fulfilling life—building great businesses for an even greater purpose.**

Thank you for embarking on this journey to elevate your business team. May the strategies and stories shared within these pages inspire you to lead with vision, forge successful teams, and make an indelible difference in the world.

Again, For those **ready to take the next step**, I am here to offer support, guidance, and coaching to help you navigate this exciting journey. **Contact me at askmj12@gmail.com or call 847-372-3432.** You can also see me on Linked In (Michael R Johnson, MATL). Let's move forward together, transforming your business for long-lasting

CONCLUSION STORY & CONTACT INFORMATION

impact and success.

Leaders also understand the value of life long learning. By my association with the Global Leadership Summit, my Master's degree and my work with fellow coaches, I had the opportunity to *learn from these great teachers. Here is the list of their books that help shape my work.* I hope you will add them to your library and refer to them as often as I do.

- *Great By Choice* by Jim Collins
- *The Seven Habits of Highly Effective People* by Stephen R. Covey
- *The Speed of Trust* by Stephen M.R. Covey
- *The Advantage* by Patrick Lencioni
- *The Five Dysfunctions of a Team* by Patrick Lencioni
- *Crucial Conversations* by Joseph Grenny, Kerry Patterson, Ron McMillan, Al Switzler, and Emily Gregory
- *Death by Meeting* by Patrick Lencioni
- *Scaling Up* by Verne Harnish
- *Traction* by Gino Wickman
- *What the Heck is EOS* by Gino Wickman and Tom Bouwer
- *Strengths Based Leadership* by Tom Rath and Barry Conchie
- *Earn It* by Jill E. Young
- *Start With Why* by Simon Sinek
- *Lessons For Living: What Only Adversity Can Teach You* by Phil Stutz
- *The Tools: 5 Tools to Help You Find Courage, Creativity, and Willpower—and Inspire You to Live Your Life in Forward Motion* by Phil Stutz and Barry Michels

Phil & Barry's title really caps off my little book. May you find the courage, creativity and willpower to fully Live!

www.ingramcontent.com/pod-product-compliance
Lightning Source LLC
Chambersburg PA
CBHW030052230526
45471CB00003B/1060